Todd Schimmell

Spark of Wonder
Poems to Ignite Young Imaginations

Spark of Wonder

Spark of Wonder
Poems to Ignite Young Imaginations

A collection of poems and illustrations
by
Todd Schimmell

Art Director
Kirsten Schimmell

Copyright © 2024 by Todd Schimmell

All rights reserved. No part of this book may be reproduced or transmitted in any form or by any means, graphic, electronic, or mechanical, including photocopying, recording, taping, or by any information storage system, without the written permission of the author or publisher except in the case of brief quotations embodied in critical articles and reviews.

a Compassio Veraque LLC imprint

ISBN: 978-1-965633-01-4

printed in the United States of America

Spark of Wonder

WELCOME

Welcome to my wild mind.
Rhyming stories is what you'll find.
This is where your thoughts run free,
Spark your creativity.
Sometimes I'll ask you to write
And draw until your hearts delight,
Or read away and wonder through.
Just know this book was made for you!

HAVE FUN!

Spark of Wonder

WORLD'S EDGE

I wandered to the world's edge,
Sticking my toes out to the ledge.
Hoping I could glimpse and see,
The future that awaits for me.
I saw a feast, but skipped a treat.
A stunning sight beneath my feet.
I looked ahead and missed somehow,
The wondrous view of here and now.

Todd Schimmell

WHAT GOES UP

I tried a science experiment today.
I thought my mom would approve.
I even included my brother Jay,
Which was a kind-hearted move.
I set out to confirm, what goes up must fall.
I gave Jay a special balloon.
He went up alright, no problem at all.
I hope he comes down soon.
He looks okay; he isn't scared,
But my mom's upset!
"The longer he's off the ground", she said,
"The longer grounding you'll get."

TIM LET IT GO

The pressure was building,
Tim thought he would burst.
A room full of people, he was dying of thirst.
So parched from nerves as he began his speech.
He opened his mouth, his voice out of reach.
No words came out, not even an "um".
Tim begged himself to eke out a hum.
He took a deep breath, soothing his mind.
Then a loud noise BOOMED from behind.
The pressure he felt...it was not tension.
Tim "Let It go" I'm sorry to mention.

Todd Schimmell

FUNKY SKUNKY

A skunk sat up high in a tree.
He wanted to be left alone.
If high enough, no one would see
him trying on cologne.
A little bit here and a little bit there,
He hoped that would do the trick.
How embarrassing to be a skunk,
whose own smell made him sick.

SPELLING BEE

I studied so hard for the spelling bee.
I learned all I could from A to Z.
Every item I have in my home,
I could spell right down to the hair on my comb.
Point at anything, I'd spell it with ease.
It's like I had a word spelling disease.
Though it didn't matter, I failed the test.
The spelling bee stung me, it wasn't impressed.

Todd Schimmell

BAILEY BROWN'S FROWN

Bailey Brown loves to furrow and frown.
She's often told to flip it around.
She's not trying to look like a frump.
A smile feels forced, her lips just slump.
She is happy with the way they sag.
She thinks it's cute and not a drag.
Smiling is common, everyone grins.
Not many can drop their lips to their chins.
She is different; it suits her well.
She smile's inside. You just can't tell.

FOOD FRIEND

With leftover food I made a friend.
I believe I picked the perfect blend.
Such a kind fellow from the start,
I hand-picked the ripest artichoke heart.
A head of lettuce to nod and agree.
Arms to hug of macaroni.
Angel hair pasta for style and grace.
Eyes of potatoes to make up his face.
Two ears of corn to hear all of my woes.
A few burger buns to fit in old clothes.
He didn't stay long. He was mush by eight.
I forgot food has to refrigerate.

Todd Schimmell

OUTWIT THE WOOSER

You can't outwit the wild Wooser.
It's too smart; you'll be the loser.
It hides in a cave, so deep and dark,
Protected by the furry Glark.
What are these creatures, you may ask?
You show me, that's your task.

*Draw the wild Wooser and furry Glark.

THE LINE

I found a line and stood there all day.
What it was for, I couldn't say?
The line was over a mile long.
So many people wouldn't be wrong.
I jumped right in; I couldn't miss out,
On what their excitement was all about.
The line started moving and moved really fast,
But many line cutters ran right past.
I tried to keep up, the line kept going.
I had to see this, THAT I was knowing.
I ran all night into the dawn,
To find out I finished a marathon!?

Todd Schimmell

COMPSOGNATHUS

The Compsognathus was a tiny creature.
Being small was its biggest feature.
As tall as a chicken, it ran in packs,
Eating up insects as savory snacks.
Some call it "compy" and shorten its name.
Removing the one big thing it could claim.
So COMPSOGNATHUS is what I will say,
And I'll mispronounce it in every way!

WEREWHAT?

The moon is full, and I feel strange.
Suddenly my body is starting to change.
But there's no need to howl and prowl.
I'd rather holler, "Owyhee Ow!"
A curly tail and pointy quills,
This Were-fail is causing chills.
I've also grown a snorty snout.
What a weird Were-turnabout.
I'm no Werewolf, what's the deal?
Here comes my big Were-reveal?
I've changed into a spiky swine!
The great Were-Porky-Porcupine!?

Todd Schimmell

CUDDLY BEAR

That bear is cuddly, don't worry, trust me.
His fur is fluffy, which means he must be.
What a sweet bear. He's clearly no threat.
   He looks friendly, I'll give him a pet.
Hmm not cuddly, and his breath is smelly.
I know this because I'm stuck in his belly.

WHO

Who, Who, Who is making that noise.
Who keeps me awake, a fact it enjoys.
Who talks all night, every time it appears.
I don't enjoy Who, Who hurts my ears.
Who doesn't care if it makes me upset.
The day I met Who is a day I regret.
Who is Who? Let me explain.
Who's an owl that loves saying its name.

Todd Schimmell

WHAT!?

I don't know what? I don't know who?
At this time, I don't have a clue.
How or why; I'm completely miffed?
This has set my mind adrift.
Where and when; oh, how to begin?
What an odd situation I am in.
I need a clue to get this started.
It seems my brain has departed.
Maybe that's what I'm looking for!
My brain has left me to explore.
It should have told me before it fled.
Now I'm confused with an empty head.

DANCE AROUND THE GLOBE

Joy dances around the globe with a twirl.
As she does her thoughts swirl.
She hopes to dance in every town,
A ballerina, well renowned.
She spins and reads every country's name,
Pretending to dance to their acclaim.
Does this help? She's yet to see,
But now she knows geography!

Todd Schimmell

BORUMP THE GIANT

For centuries giants got a bad rap.
They'd stomp and destroy towns into scrap.
It wasn't because they were nasty and mean,
Giants were big, the towns were unseen.
Borump Gloober was the first to see,
Finally looking below his knee.
He crushed a house, but no one was there.
Borump knew he must treat this with care.
He grabbed his hammer and nails to rebuild.
When the family got home, they were more than thrilled.
The house he built was twice the size,
With a big sign made for giant eyes.
A warning to all, to watch where they clomp,
"Protected by Borump, giants NO STOMP!"

Spark of Wonder

EW, THE EWE

Ew the Ewe ate an interesting stew.
Made from the garden she planted and grew.
It wasn't your average corn and beans.
You wouldn't want this by any means.
Let's just say she's "Ew" for a reason.
The plants she chooses aren't ever in season.
Have you ever heard of Grumpily Stocks?
It resembles the taste of dirty old socks.
How about Red Kipperbell Clots?
The ones with gray and purple spots?
Brown Ploppy is another addition.
The name says it all, the smell I won't mention.
That's just three of the mixture she grows.
Even Ew has to pinch her own nose.
She prepares the fire and adds her plants,
Then begins her wafting dance.
She does this so it's safe to play.
Those awful smells keep wolves away!

Todd Schimmell

EVERYTHING MUST GO

"Everything must go, you see!?"
Hollered Gage McFlowery.
He'll sell anything for cash,
From beauty cream to neighbor's trash.
It doesn't matter what or who,
If it's old, worn, or new.
Do you want it? Gage cares not.
He'll simply ask, "How much you got?"
Nothing's off limits, it's all for sale.
You can buy his house, every single nail.
Gage wants things gone, but none know why.
He sells his thoughts to all who try.

BLANK CANVAS

A blank canvas is the most exciting.
It waits for you warm and inviting.
What to do? What path to take?
Thoughtful or silly for silliness sake?
Paint it bright colors or pencil it in?
Make straight lines or ones that spin?
Glue all the pieces or pull them apart?
What's most important is that you start.

*Take out a piece of paper and a pen/pencil. Put the pen/pencil on the paper and see what happens!

Todd Schimmell

CATCH A STAR

I'm done making wishes on a star.
Saying, "I wish" doesn't get me far.
If stars are the reason dreams come true,
Waiting isn't what I should do.
It's time to create a brand-new plan,
Run and jump, as high as I can.
Grab that star and hold on tightly,
If I miss, I'll repeat it nightly.
As long as there's a star to shine,
I'll keep reaching until it's mine!

RHYMING BUSINESS

I'm in the rhyming business as you can tell.
I write poems that rhyme for books I sell.
For me it's worked out well to rhyme,
But that's not true all of the time.
Just ask my friend Remy McBeth,
Quilts on stilts scares her to death.

Todd Schimmell

RAIN CLOUDS

The clouds ruined my day of fun.
Of things I planned, wet wasn't one.
They've muddied up my space to play,
Without giving me a say.
I sprayed them with a garden hose,
Such a strange response I chose.
I don't believe the clouds got wet,
But they knew I was upset.

PIGGY BANK

I have a trusty piggy bank,
And love it when the coins go clank.
The one I bought I have to smash,
In order to get out my cash.
I saved, I earned, and now it's time,
To bust out every single dime.
Though a hammer I will not swing,
I've grown to love that piggy thing.
It grins and grins as change goes in,
So instead, I'll shake and spin.
It's getting dizzy stroke by stroke,
But dizzy sure beats being broke.

GREATEST POEM

I wrote the greatest poem ever.
It was delightful, witty, and clever.
It's a story I wish I could tell,
Though I don't remember it well.
You'd love to hear it, I think?
But I wrote it down with invisible ink.

TREE OF KNOWLEDGE

I learned something new from the Knowledge Tree,
A lesson forced and given to me.
I learned about luck, bumps, and gravity,
And how I'm not happy with all of those three.
This bump on my head, I didn't foresee.
Apples CAN fall far from the tree.

EGG IN A TREE

The egg was cracked, the tree was bare,
The boy was climbing without a care.
When he saw the egg, he held it tight.
He hugged and loved with all his might.
In a blink, the boy felt pride,
Compelled to save what was inside.
He stayed all night wrapped up and curled,
Being needed changed his world.

Todd Schimmell

SMILE MORE

Smile more, doesn't that sound simple.
Grin so much your cheeks fold and dimple.
Bring the happy, show off your giggle.
Dance and laugh, shake and wiggle!
Pass it along like a common cold,
To everyone, young and old.
Then all will have smiles on their face.
Wouldn't this world be a better place?

GET DRESSED

My alarm went off, but my eyes stayed shut.
I was groggy and in a rut.
I felt for my clothes and got myself dressed.
I clearly needed some extra rest.
At breakfast I made eggs and steak,
But wasn't ready to be awake.
I got confused when I took a bite.
I unzipped my pants...
That didn't seem right!?

Todd Schimmell

CANDLE

The candle flame went this way and that.
It danced like no one was watching.
In awe I took a closer look,
and almost blew it out coughing.
It flickered and flashed a silent ballet
as it leaped to and fro.
Then went out with a roll of smoke.
Oh, what a dazzling show.

GOOD CLUCK

Rooster wakes up to put on his show,
Thinking he makes the whole world go.
He waves to tell the Moon goodbye.
He buttons his shirt, and fixes his tie.
When the Sun peeks out, the spotlight is on,
It's time to sing his roosterly song.
He takes his stage, a wooden fencepost;
Ready to do what he loves the most!
He clears his throat, he starts his call,
"COCK-A-DOODLE DO!!!" to one and all.
His job is done, he goes back to bed.
A full day's work, at least in his head.

Todd Schimmell

HAIR STARE

Both are amazing in what they can grow.
The best mustache and hair that they know.
They stare at each other wanting more.
Where they are rich, they only see poor.
Respect what is great in others that's true,
But don't forget what is great about you.

MYTHICAL BEASTS

I'm not afraid of mythical beasts.
They do not scare me in the least.
A jackalope looks super sweet,
To meet one would be really neat.
Another thing I'd love to do,
Is play sasquatch peek a boo.
Then nap inside a griffin's nest.
I hear they're soft and just the best.
I'd even stroll with a lonesome troll.
I say these things because I know,
They're all pretend and don't exist.
So any fears can be dismissed.
What kind of beast can you create?
Go on, start thinking, don't you wait!

*Draw and write about your own mythical beast.

Todd Schimmell

EVENING ERMA

Bedtimes exist for everyone's safety.
I say this in fact, I'm not being hasty.
Kids may ask for an extra hour,
Don't give in, they might go sour.
Don't believe me? Here's a tale,
Of Evening Erma's parent fail.
Erma's bedtime was promptly at nine,
But some nights her parents would lose track of time.
They'd know their mistake by nine o' five,
When Evening Erma would come alive!
She'd stomp through the house sleepy and mean,
Thrashing and smashing everything seen.
Her family tries to avoid her path,
Even her father is scared of her wrath.
At about 10 she'll crash fast asleep.
They tuck her in bed and don't make a peep,
Then clean up everything that she broke.
A warning to all: bedtime is no joke!

DRAGON CAT

Dragon Cat's a lazy beast.
When doing tasks, he does the least.
He's a dragon who never fights,
No epic battles with jousting knights.
He has no riches to hold or guard,
Protecting gold would be too hard.
He has wings, but rarely flaps,
Except to fan while taking naps.
He eats his meals lukewarm or cold,
He won't breathe fire, truth be told.
It takes too long to get that hot.
So, a little smoke is all he's got.

CAPTAIN FINEAS

Captain Fineas led his ship.
His crew followed orders without any lip.
"There's a storm-a-brewing, all hands-on deck,
I won't lose a man; you heard me correct!
Hoist the mainsail, we're in for a fight!
The weather looks rough, but we'll be alright."
They knew this was true, and I'll tell you why.
The ship was on land, no water close by.

TOOT MY OWN HORN

I would play you the greatest song.
Not a single toot would be wrong.
You would know you're hearing the best.
I'd leave you amazed and impressed.
You'd hang on every note,
Cuz I'm the trumpeting G.O.A.T.
But it's too bad I've sworn,
To never toot my own horn.

LOUDMOUTH MIME

You can always tell what he'll do next.
The Loudmouth Mime isn't complex.
He shouts his routine and spoils the guess.
You can't look away at his awful mess.
If anyone says that's not what mimes do,
He claims his miming is perfect and true.
When asked to explain and give reasons why,
He suddenly quiet and starts being shy.

EXIT

Where is the exit, I'd like to leave.
I can't find a single sign I believe.
One says this way, the other says that.
I'm currently stuck right where I'm at,
Cuz I won't move til I know what's right.
I've bumped into every wall in sight.
I shouldn't have entered this terrible store.
They sell Exit signs from floor to floor.
The only way out is buying a sign.
What a remarkably sneaky design!

SNACK ATTACK

Late at night my belly rumbles.
I need a snack to cure the grumbles.
My kitchen is dark, who knows what's hiding?
Things look different without the lighting.
I need to look mean. I need to be tough.
I'll admit I'm scared but learned a bluff.
I go to sleep in karate clothes.
I taught myself kicks and a ninja pose.
So far, it's worked. I'm alone as can be.
If something is there, it's more scared of me!

'ITCHY SWEATER' MOOD

I feel fussy. I can't say it better.
It's like I'm stuck in an itchy sweater.
I want to be happy; it's so confusing.
This isn't the feeling I would be choosing.
What do I do with this itchy mood?
A mood that wants to so rudely intrude.
Can I remove it, where do I start?
It seems to be stuck. It's glued to my heart.
I may need some help; could you do me a favor?
Draw me a smile to change my behavior.
You can use your finger, pencil, or pen.
Anything works, just get me to grin!
Itchy moods can be defeated.
By placing smiles wherever they're needed.

MR. FINNEGAN

Mr. Finnegan turned young again.
He found the Fountain of Youth.
He took a swim, turned twelve again.
I swear, it's the honest truth.
He was so upset he swam too long.
He meant to be twenty-two.
Now he's repeating the seventh grade
and will sadly have to make do.

THREAD

I found a thread, the tiniest string.
It could belong to anything.
I pulled and pulled, it just kept going.
With every pull suspense was growing.
Nothing else mattered, I have to admit.
The more it unraveled, the more I'd commit.
Just when I thought my answer was near?
More and more threads would seem to appear.
What a weird puzzle I find myself solving.
I do believe this thing is dissolving.
What will be left? Will I find out?
What this unraveling's all about?
At last, I see the end of the string!
It's attached to…Well, nothing?
I thought I'd be sad but instead I feel silly.
It's a string to my pants, now I'm just chilly.

Todd Schimmell

NOT LION

Have you noticed I'm lion? I am by the way.
In all that I do and all that I say.
I'm about to snack, and I'd love you to join.
I'm making a sandwich, a tenderloin.
Two pieces of bread, a slice of cheese,
My secret sauce, but just a squeeze.
Oh no, my meat! It's been misplaced.
But I'm lion, just look at my face.
Can you help me look? Step a bit nearer.
You'll see that I'm lion, I can't make this clearer.
Here's the deal, if you've yet to conclude.
I've misspelled lyin' to make YOU, my food!

RHINOCERFISH

Deep in the sea it swims and storms.
Charging fishpoles with boney horns.
It cuts the lines, it can't be caught,
That's why they are so hard to spot.
No blinking or you'll probably miss,
The overlooked rhinocerfish!

*Draw a brand-new animal by combining at least two other animals. Now, write about what your new animal can do.

Todd Schimmell

CLOWN IS KOI

Something seems false to my eyes.
One clown is dressed in a silly disguise.
The hair seems out of place,
As well as the big round nose on its face.
It's not being bashful or shy.
But that clown is koi, you can't deny.

I DON'T NEED NO HAIR

"I don't need no hair!" said George Sinclair,
Although he cared his head was bare.
He used to have long locks he cherished.
When it fell out, George got embarrassed.
He bought wigs but they always felt wrong.
So, George grew his beard out extra-long.
He took his comb and swished and swooshed.
George was proud of what he produced.
He thought to himself, "No one will know."
George now had a confident glow.
Everyone could tell his hair was fake.
Though all kept quiet for George's sake.

Todd Schimmell

ONE MILLION WISHES

I caught a Genie who gave me one wish.
I asked for one million more wishes with this.
To my surprise he agreed without question,
Although I must make a regretful confession.
The wishes are great, those I'm enjoying.
But this Genie won't leave, and he's awfully annoying.
Getting all I want should've been fun,
Except for privacy of that I have none.

MAYOR

Jean was on stage before the debate,
Tidying up while the candidates wait.
The crowd grew quiet as she swept the floor.
Then people shouted, "WE WANT MORE!"
"She's got my vote, what a great plan!"
"She'll clean up the city, I'm a big fan!"
Jean was confused, "I'm not running for mayor?"
She tried to explain, but the crowd didn't care.
The candidates spoke, but they were ignored.
The crowd wanted Jean; they all cheered and ROARED!!!
What a chain of events, unforeseen and rare.
Jean went on stage and left the new Mayor!

CHRIS CROSS APPLESAUCE

When Becky Sue said sit next to me.
Something happened Chris didn't foresee.
His palms got sweaty, and his mind went blank.
He lost every thought, and his poor heart sank.
He forgot how to sit. What should he do?
Chris looked around, his options were few.
Nothing made sense, but he had to move.
Chris went to the ground with something to prove.
He stumbled face first and felt all the feels.
Chris had fallen head over heels.

BIPPUS AND BAGGETT

Bippus and Baggett were two lonely elves,
Who hated each other and hated themselves.
They hated the bushes, they hated the trees,
They hated the patches of hair on their knees.
They hated the sun for the dryness and heat,
But yelled at the rain when it dampened their feet!
They'd spend their days hating all that they'd do.
Every minute past, present, and new.
Now, Bippus and Baggett, chose to be dreary.
I tell you this tale in hopes you'll be leery.
What you choose affects your view.
Don't let Bippus and Baggett be you!

Todd Schimmell

*A few words make a difference in how we feel. I've taken out the negative words so you can add positive words to make Bippus and Baggett smile.

BIPPUS AND BAGGETT

Bippus and Baggett were two ____ elves,
Who ____ each other and ____ themselves.
They ____ the bushes, they ____ the trees,
They ____ the patches of hair on their knees.
They ____ the sun for the dryness and heat,
But ____ at the rain when it dampened their feet!
They'd spend their days ____ all that they'd do.
Every minute past, present, and new.
Now, Bippus and Baggett, chose to be ____.
I tell you this tale in hopes you'll be ____.
What you choose affects your view.
____ let Bippus and Baggett be you!

MY BLANKET

It's not just a blanket, don't call it a cover.
It's a powerful item unlike any other.
It makes me feel safe, alone in the dark.
I hold on tight, and it lights a spark.
Its torn cuz its loved, a bit tattered and stained.
It has a smell that can't be explained.
But my blanket keeps me okay.
When I need a snuggle or have a bad day.

ARROW

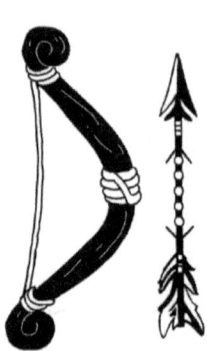

When an arrow gets formed, it's shiny and new.
It's placed in a quiver, awaiting debut.
But what is an arrow without a bow?
Something to guide it, and make it go.
The journey starts when the arrow's released.
Aiming is done and the speed is increased.
The hope is that the bow's done enough.
To send the arrow through difficult stuff.
If the arrow gets broken, bent, or stuck.
It can be shot again til the target's struck.
As long as the arrow has a bow.
There's no limit to where it can go.

Todd Schimmell

READ THE ROOM

Books as far as the eye can see.
Ready to be read by my friend and me!
Where do we start? Left, right, or middle?
Scary, funny, or ones that riddle?
Should we team up or keep to ourselves?
Read them slow, or speed through the shelves?
No matter how we wish to consume,
There's no wrong way to read the room!

THIS SIDE

Come on over, it's time to play.
This magic can take your cares away.
Step on This Side and look around.
Turn what was real upside down.
Make the grass blue or paint the sky pink.
You can do whatever you think.
On This Side the rules are your own.
The only limit is the unknown.
This Side is alive, but not without you.
Imagine all of the things you can do!

Todd Schimmell

THE MIGHTY LEAF

When leaves fall from a tree, one by one.
It's not the end, there's more to be done.
They belong to a cycle endlessly churning.
Not fearing the fall, with each season's turning.
Once on the ground their new job begins.
Feeding the tree's soil, roots, and limbs.
They are more than a leaf; they are the tree.
As long as it stands, forever they'll be.

FALLING

Am I jumping up or falling down?
As you read, I spin around.
Should I duck or take a seat?
What comes first, my head or feet?
I should be dizzy but feel fine.
I stay stuck here by design.
When you a need a friendly ear,
Come talk to me. I'll be right here.

Todd Schimmell

BRAVE SIR PHILLIP

Brave Sir Phillip is a chicken knight,
But he isn't "chicken" let's get that right.
Don't call him "yellow"; he's never scared.
He's a chicken knight, who's well prepared.
When he wakes up, he dawns his attire,
Made of cardboard and chicken wire.
He protects his coop from dangers unknown,
Creatures who try to catch chickens alone.
Not on his watch he shoos them away,
Swinging his sword made of Timothy Hay.
His sword doesn't hurt, but it tickles a lot.
Tying foes bellies in a comical knot.
They laugh so hard, they can no longer breathe,
And out of breath they'd turn and leave.
With Brave Sir Phillip standing tall.
The chicken knight for one and all!

QUICKSAND

Maci dreamed of running fast.
Faster than a cannon's blast.
A running cap, new sneakers too,
She knew her dream would soon come true.
She thought she picked the perfect ground.
Where she could break the speed of sound.
She took her mark ready to go,
But Maci started sinking slow.
She couldn't move at all because,
She didn't know what quicksand was.
She read the sign but read it wrong.
Now she'll be here all day long.

Todd Schimmell

PLANT

It starts with seeds and dirty hands,
To till up the ground and prepare the lands.
Sunlight, water, and a lot of love;
The seeds sprout roots and leaves above.
Creation's wonder begins to loom.
The magic unfolds as flowers bloom.
Ideas can start just as these seeds.
Help them to grow and see where it leads.

*Draw and write about what these seeds will grow.

SWIM THE ATLANTIC

I'm going to swim the Atlantic.
I have my gear and food.
Nothing is going to stop me.
That's my attitude.
On the count of ten I'll begin,
And start my swimming quest.
Do you believe I'll make it?
You think I'll win this test?
You do!? Fantastic!
Since there isn't any doubt.
If we both know I can,
I'll sit this one out...

UNNECESSARY FAIRY

A Tooth Fairy leaves coins and cash.
Fairy Godmother's royal ball crash.
Then there's fairies that get to delight,
Doing laundry, dishes, and deeds overnight.
All kinds of fairies spread joy with their magic.
Then there is me, my job is so tragic.
What I do seems unnecessary.
I dry drool from pillows with rags I carry.
It's not all bad. I have wings and can fly.
Just help me out kids, keep your pillows dry.

OUT OF THIS WORLD

Be creative with a pen and pad.
Write and draw about dreams you've had.
Let thoughts float free into space.
What you think up is your very own place.
Soon your mind will soar to the moon.
Fly out of this world and back by noon.

Todd Schimmell

CAN'T WAIT

How much longer should he wait?
He can't believe this is his fate.
He makes sitting down an exercise.
With bouncing feet and shaky thighs.
Watching hands move on his watch.
Counting seconds notch by notch.
He's impatient and not amused.
He only wants to be excused.
(Hurry turn the page!)

PARCHED PRINCIPAL

Miss Scuttle needed something to drink.
She couldn't speak the words she'd think.
Her mouth was dry so she grabbed a glass,
Forgetting she was in science class.
Now her thirst is no longer of note.
The drink she took left a frog in her throat.
The Frog's okay I hear it "Ribbit."
We are laughing, Miss Scuttle isn't.

Todd Schimmell

ONE TOUGH LEMON

When life hands you lemons, make lemonade,
But there's many more lemony things to be made.
Lemon pie, lemon strudel, gooey lemon bars,
Lemon cream, lemon jelly; filled up in jars.
Lemon soaps, shampoos, the list goes on...
There's many ways sour days can be won.
Making lemonade isn't enough.
When life hands you lemons, show it your tough!

MOCKINGBIRD

I tried to mock a mockingbird.
Looking back that seems absurd.
Now that bird won't let me be.
It mocks and mocks constantly.
It repeats the words I say,
And does it in an awful way.
If I'm quiet, it doesn't care.
It will mock the things I wear.
Certain things should not be done.
Mocking birds will count as one.

Todd Schimmell

MONSTER FOOD

This food I make is not for me.
It is disgusting as can be.
It's for that thing under my bed,
I need to keep it fat and fed.
It gives me recipes to keep,
So it won't eat me when I sleep.
I don't enjoy the smell and crunch,
But it's better than being lunch.

TRICK OR TREAT

Trick or Treat are the choices to make.
The answer is clear for goodness sake.
Give us candy and we will move on.
The tricks you don't want. You want us gone.
I'm not that bad, but have you met my friends?
Candy is the only safe way this ends.

TURKEY DAY

We celebrate Thanksgiving Day with loved ones near and far.
A time of togetherness no matter who you are.
Some call it, "Turkey Day" but the turkeys take offense.
The day AFTER they celebrate.
For them it makes more sense.

SELFIE THE ELFIE

Selfie The Elfie works in Santa's Shop.
He's supposed to be a toy maker.
You can often hear his camera click.
He's a constant selfie taker.
Don't be surprised on Christmas Day
if you get an extra prize.
Selfie thinks his photos
will be pleasing to your eyes.

1000 WAYS THAT DIDN'T WORK

I've tried 1000 ways that didn't work.
The answer's here, I feel it lurk.
Some may just accept defeat,
But that'd be wrong, it's not complete.
Why give up on progress made?
So many tries and simply fade.
I know that I can get this done.
Here goes attempt 1001!

NEW HAT

I was overjoyed to get a new hat.
My old one was bent and broken at that.
A brand-new hat is as good as it gets.
I wanted to try it to see how it fits.
Never mind, just forget what I said.
During the excitement I've lost my head.

SOCK LEFT

I'm missing my left sock or maybe my right?
I had a pair in my drawer nice and tight.
Now for some reason I only have one.
Where on earth could my sock have gone?
Surely it didn't just get up and walk?
For crying out loud it's a silly old sock!
My shoes stuck around, but geez are they stinking.
That's why my sock left, now that I'm thinking!

Todd Schimmell

THE BOX

I found a box sealed up shut.
Something's inside, I don't know what.
My mind is racing. I want to look.
Is it a wizard's sorcery book?
What if it's secrets about to be told,
Of a treasure map that leads to gold.
It could be a feast of delicious grub.
Or a genie's lamp that needs a rub?
Perhaps a beast, one of a kind.
These are the things that come to mind.
If it's opened, the truth will be seen.
So I keep it shut to guess and dream.

*Draw what you think is inside the box.
Write all about this newfound thing.

POLITE KNIGHT'S OATH

Battle hard, but be polite.
Don't give in, keep up the fight.
It may get scary and full of fright.
Be brave, be bold, and do what's right.
Defend the weak, they need your might.
Let your kindness be the light.
No weapons needed, it's alright.
A smile's your sword, good sir knight.

Todd Schimmell

STARE OFF

I'm in a stare off with a worthy foe.
We started playing long ago.
I'm tired, but it doesn't show.
Or if it does, he's not said so.
When will this end? I do not know?
But he won't move, so I won't go.

WOOLF

Leonard is a wolf who's more wrong than right.
He thinks he's sneaky, but always in sight.
He tries to outsmart the sheep in the flocks,
By wearing wool sweaters, with matching socks.
This wolf in sheep's clothing is easy to view.
The tags on his clothes would be the first clue.
If that's not enough to set him apart.
Leonard loves sweaters with tacky art.

Todd Schimmell

LOVE-A-BULL LLAMA

Love a bull Llama, he's trying hard.
Love a bull Llama, let down your guard.
Love a bull Llama, he's brought you roses.
Love a bull Llama, he's painted his toeses.
Love a bull Llama, he wants to be friends.
Love a bull Llama, look how he grins.
Love a bull Llama, he's just like you.
Love a bull Llama, he's lovable too!

NOW O' CLOCK

Tick Tock there's too much to be done.
So many things one after one.
Should I wish for a clock to stop time?
To pause and make every second mine?
I'd do it all, while clocks stay still,
But I don't think I'd like how that'd feel?
Seconds tick away, it gives me intent.
To laugh, and love; It's time well spent.
I can't look back on what could've been,
Or wish away the day I'm in.
I continue to say, "One day I might?"
NOW is the time to prove myself right!

Todd Schimmell

INSPIRATION

What's in this bottle will lift your spirit.
It could change your life just standing near it.
One spritz is all you will ever need,
To chase your wildest dreams indeed.
What's inside? I'm glad you inquired.
It's filled with hope! Go be inspired!

ICE CREAM

I ordered ice cream on a stick.
It started melting really quick.
I grabbed a bowl and ate it fast,
Knowing that it might not last.
To my surprise no drops were spilled.
But my head, it nearly killed.
My brain froze, lips went astray.
Now my face is stuck this way.

WISHFUL THINKING

I was thinking a thought, about what I forgot?
An idea for a poem? Maybe or not?
It was right there on the edge of my brain.
Now it's just out of reach; I'm going insane.
This could have been it, my best story to date,
But my mind let it go, and my pen was too late.
Before I give up, I'll think really hard.
Now I recall but please disregard.
Here is the uneventful twist.
I needed milk on my grocery list.

Todd Schimmell

HARD HEAD ED

His head is the biggest and hardest around.
Poor Ed can't keep his head off the ground.
But he'll never ask for help to his feet.
He's the most stubborn Ed you will meet.
He'll try all day long to get up on his own,
Making his troubles to others unknown.
Instead of receiving a helping hand.
He'll lay there all day and pretend it was planned.

WUZZLEHUNKS

I met tiny creatures in my backyard.
This sighting took us both off guard.
They told me they were Wuzzlehunks.
They had antennas and big, long trunks.
They live underground, and now and then,
Surface to play and soak the sun in.
They normally go unseen by most.
Their lookout had fallen asleep on post.
Today I'm one of the lucky few.
Who gets to see what Wuzzlehunks do.

*Draw a Wuzzlehunk, and write down what you think Wuzzlehunks do.

GYM TIME

I've heard that working out is rough.
I've found it not to be that tough.
The trick is having a good routine.
I've discovered one I've never seen.
I enjoy my gym time now.
I'll let you know my secret how.
I don't lift weights, just things I bake.
Now working out's a piece of cake!

HIDE AND SEEK

It's a friendly game of hide and seek.
It doesn't matter if they peek.
They play out in a giant field.
There's not much there to hide or shield.
Except for one shady tree.
No need to seek that's where they'll be.
They climb on limbs; the tree don't mind.
Here, true friends aren't hard to find.

Todd Schimmell

RALPH AND RIDDY

Ralph and Riddy are starving to death.
Giggling so hard they can't catch their breath.
The food is right there, they could eat with ease,
But can't stop laughing, Ralph cut the cheese.

ELEPHANT IN THE ROOM

Excuse me, I have something to say.
Unless I address it, it won't go away.
I know it's odd, and everyone's staring.
But left alone it's overbearing.
I won't sit silent and just assume,
That the elephant leaves the room.

PINATA

No, you will not take a swing,
Not a single whack.
Please just go away,
And don't you dare come back.
I will stand right here,
Forever in your way.
You won't convince me not to,
What did you just say?
This thing is full of candy?
Allow me to step aside.
Would you like some help,
Getting what's inside?

Todd Schimmell

_NO_MAN

My snowman's a _no_man,
Things are disappearing.
I figured he would melt,
That's what I was fearing.
His hat and scarf are gone.
His nose is an empty notch.
I now stand on guard,
With my trusty dog on watch.
I'm so glad he's here.
He brought me a scarf and hat.
Also sticks for fetching,
While we wait and sat.
He even brought a carrot.
He's made me full and cozy.
Just one slight complaint,
The carrot tastes nosey.

LOST MY MARBLES

There's been a misunderstanding.
My words need a bit more expanding.
I've not lost my mind or my head.
But it sounds like that's what I said.
I've lost my marbles but I'm okay.
They spilled on the floor and rolled away.

CHARITY IS RICH

She seems pretty bold
by the name on that box,
and awfully convincing when she talks.
She never says what donations are for.
Only that she could surely use more.
She's raised lots of money,
but it's a shame.
I've caught on to her fund-raising game.
I'm rarely one to tattle or snitch,
But Charity's a person,
and she's getting rich.

Todd Schimmell

NOT SO FAST FRIENDS

The turtle sat on his rock alone.
He wanted a friend to call his own.
He asked a bird to visit and play.
The bird didn't answer; it flew away.
He turned to a fish but moved too slow.
The fish was swimming and on the go.
The turtle was sad til it saw a snail,
Hanging out with a matching shell.

They talked all day long and as the sun set.
They went to shake hands but still haven't met.

WILL THE WIZARD

Will joined a wizard's class.
He isn't catching on that fast.
His wand, his hat, all look the part.
But wizardry is not his art.
When he tries a "zap-a-roo",
His wand lets out a spark or two.
It's good for popcorn on the cob,
But that's about the only job.

SALLY LOUISE

Sally Louise put cheese on her knees.
She did this every day.
Monday was Cheddar. Tuesday was Swiss.
Wednesday was Monterey.
Thursday was Bleu. Friday was Feta.
Saturday was Colby Jack.
On Sunday, her choice was Mozzarella,
Her all-time favorite snack.

SEAL OF APPROVAL

I traveled to find where I belong.
You wouldn't believe the places I've gone.
North to South Pole and all in between.
Deserts, oceans, and meadows of green.
Along the way, I drew a doodle,
And made what I needed, my seal of approval.

*Draw your own "seal of approval" and write some encouraging words.

STRESS BALLOON

If you're feeling stressed, pretend you're a balloon.
Pay attention to the air you consume.
Remember if you have too much you can pop.
Let your air out if you want it to stop.
By doing things that make you feel happy,
Like singing, dancing, or taking a nappy.
Soon that balloon filling with stress,
Will deflate and not burst in a mess.

Todd Schimmell

OUTER SPACE

What's out there in outer space?
A never-ending wondrous place.
So much to view, so much to see.
To look beyond the galaxy.
Aliens in flying ships?
Galactic sharks with smiling lips?
Who knows what's really there to find.
Your guess would be as good as mine.
At night look up and make a scene.
Connect the stars and in between.

*Close your eyes and picture a night's sky.
Write and draw what you might see beyond the stars.

Spark of Wonder

Not only do I write and draw books, but I also get to serve and protect my community as a School Resource Officer. I love being a "Hero Protector"!

HERO PROTECTOR(SRO)

I'm the cop in your school every day.
We laugh, make jokes, and play.
You give me high fives, hugs, and hellos,
But I want you to know how far this goes.
When I came to your school I became more,
A mentor, protector, teacher, I swore,
To keep you safe and guide your hand.
Allowing life to move as it's planned.
I stop the threat outside and within.
But you're the heroes about to begin,
To change the world and make it better.
Til' then I'm here as the hero protector.

Todd Schimmell

THE GUARD

Halt, who's there? I'm the guard of this book.
  Don't turn the page. Don't take a look.

I'm trying to stop what happens next.
By keeping your eyes away from the text.
  I'm your protector here to defend...

Oh no, you turned it. This is the end.
GOODBYE

INDEX

#
1000 Ways That Didn't Work p.75

A
Arrow p.56

B
Baily Brown p.11
Bippus And Baggett p.54
Blank Canvas p.24
Borump The Giant p.21
Brave Sir Phillip p.61

C
Captain Fineas p.39
Candle p.33
Can't Wait p.67
Catch A Star p.25
Charity Is Rich p.92
Chris Cross Applesauce p.53
Clown Is Koi p.49
Compsognathus p.15
Cuddly Bear p.17

D
Dance Around The Globe p.20
Dragon Cat p.38

E
Egg In A Tree p.30
Elephant In The Room p.89
Evening Erma p.37
Everything Must Go p.23
Ewe, The Ewe p.22

Exit p.42

F
Falling p.60
Food Friend p.12
Funky Skunky p.9

G
Get Dressed p.32
Good Cluck p.34
Greatest Poem p.29
Gym Time p.87

H
Hair Stare p.35
Hard Head Ed p.85
Hide And Seek p.88

I
I Don't Need No Hair p.50
Ice Cream p.83
Inspiration p.83
'Itchy Sweater' Mood p.44

L
Lost My Marbles p.82
Love-A-Bull Llama p.81
Loudmouth Mime p.41

M
Mayor p.52
Mocking Bird p.70
Monster Food p.71
Mr. Finnegan p.45
My Blanket p.56
Mythical Beast p.36

N
New Hat p.76
_No_Man p.91
Not Lion p.47
Not So Fast Friends p.93
Now O' Clock p.82

O
One Million Wishes p.51
One Tough Lemon p.69
Out Of This World p.66
Outer Space p.97
Outwit The Wooser p.13

P
Parched Principal p.68
Piggy Bank p.28
Pinata p.90
Plant p.63
Polite Knight p.78

Q
Quicksand p.62

R
Rain Clouds p.27
Ralph And Riddy p.89
Read The Room p.57
Rhinocerfish p.48
Rhyming Business p.26

S
Sally Louise p.95
Seal Of Approval p.96
Selfie The Elfie p.74
Smile More p.31

Snack Attack p.43
Sock Left p.76
SRO(Hero Protector) p.98
Stare Off p.79
Stress Balloon p.96
Swim The Atlantic p.64

T
Tim Let It Go p.8
Thread p.46
The Box p.77
The Guard p.99
The Line p.14
The Mighty Leaf p.59
This Side p.58
Toot My Own Horn p.40
Tree Of Knowledge p.29
Trick Or Treat p.72
Turkey Day p.73

U
Unnecessary Fairy p.65

W
Welcome p.5
Werewhat? p.16
What Goes Up p.7
Who p.18
What!? p.19
Will The Wizard p.94
Wishful Thinking p.84
Woolf p.80
World's Edge p.6
Wuzzlehunks p.86

Todd Schimmell is a happily married father of four and an award-winning school resource officer in Southern Indiana. All Todd Schimmell books are available on Amazon

Other Todd Schimmell picture book titles.

KIDS' COMPASS SERIES

Book One 'The Elephant Tooted'

Book Two 'Carl The Chameleon'

Book Three 'Bear Says Quack'

Book Four 'The Curious Troll'

Book Five 'What Can This Shrew Do?'

Book Six 'The Land Of Ish'

Book Seven 'Why Is The Stegosaurus Dancing?'

Book Eight 'Unruly Bully'

Book Nine 'But I'm A Crocodile'

Book Ten 'Crab Shell For Sale'

Book Eleven 'Fennec Finds His Voice'

LET'S BE SILLY SERIES

Book One 'The Book That Stunk'

Book Two 'The Fun Reader'

Book Three 'Boogers Are Not Food (And Other Helpful Tips)

Spark of Wonder

www.ingramcontent.com/pod-product-compliance
Lightning Source LLC
LaVergne TN
LVHW051847080426
835512LV00018B/3108